CW00821262

EXMOOR
A WINTER'S TALE

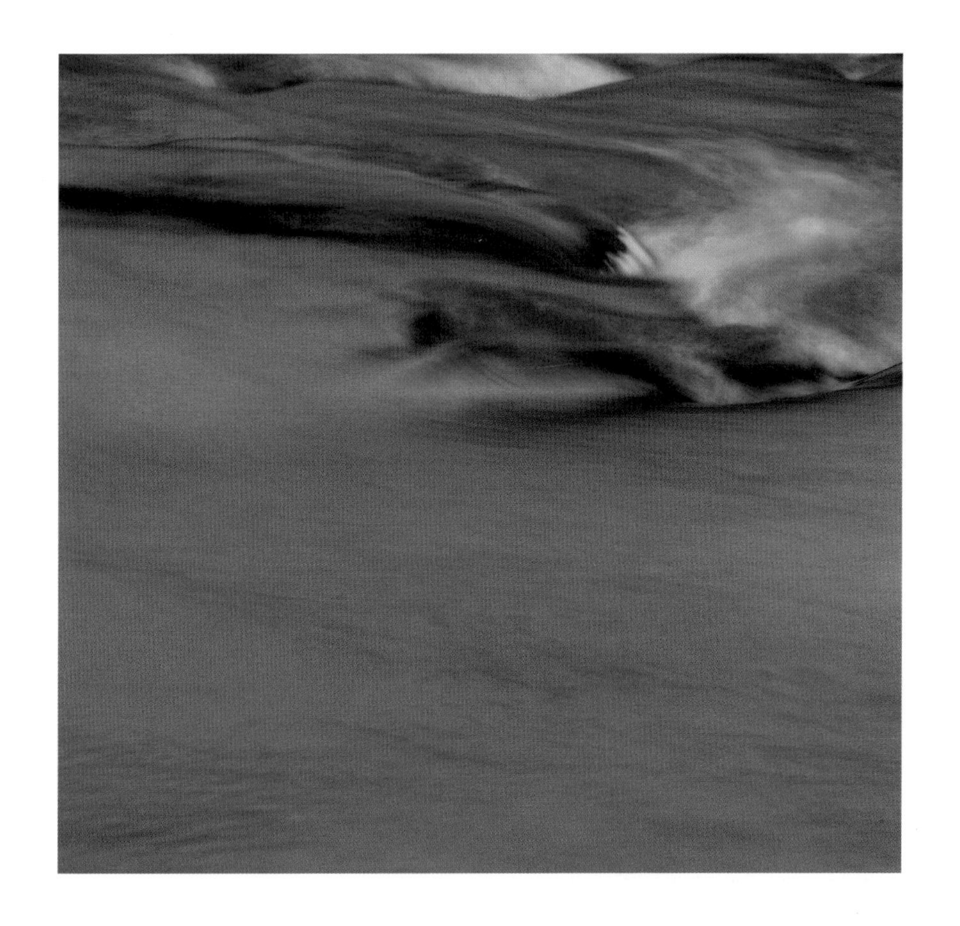

NEVILLE STANIKK

HALSGROVE

First published in Great Britain in 2009

Title page photograph:
Reflections of sunlight on the River Barle (detail)

British Library Cataloguing-in-Publication Data
A CIP record for this title is available from the British Library

ISBN 978 1 84114 927 1

HALSGROVE
Halsgrove House,
Ryelands Industrial Estate,
Bagley Road, Wellington, Somerset TA21 9PZ
Tel: 01823 653777 Fax: 01823 216796
email: sales@halsgrove.com

Part of the Halsgrove group of companies
Information on all Halsgrove titles is available at: www.halsgrove.com

Printed and bound in India on behalf of JFDi Print Services Ltd

INTRODUCTION

When I accepted the commission for this book I had no idea that it would let me experience the passage of winter in a way that few people get to do in modern times, and that it would show me a Christmas that I hadn't known for forty years.

I knew this book had to have snow and I was worried about not missing the five minutes of it that I was expecting. Little did I know that this winter would oblige with more snow than there's been for twenty years. But then little did I know that there'd be so much of it that it would take three days to get across the moors and many landmarks that I'd hoped to photograph in the snow would simply be inaccessible, not just to me but to Land Rovers or even tractors.

I have been privileged to actually experience the days shorten and then lengthen, the temperatures dip and then rise, the plant life die and then re-emerge, and to gain a feeling of winter that only someone of the past might have felt.

And until I inadvertently made my Christmas out of all the events I visited in the course of photographing this book, instead of just trudging around overheated shops and spending money, I had no idea of how Christmas had slipped out of my hands, in fact out of all our hands. If you're out amongst blue and darkness and cold, then the simple joy of small oases of orange and yellow and warmth becomes evident.

This book begins with the deepening gloom of winter and ends with the light and life of spring but at its heart is the Christmas I accidentally discovered, epitomised by the picture of the Yarnmarket at Dunster (page 35) during the two evenings of Dunster by Candlelight. As part of the festivities, a couple watch musicians perform but the parallel with a Nativity scene is uncanny. It was a picture I wasn't looking for. As all photographers are urged to do, I looked behind me and there it was. I managed one shot and then it was gone.

It would have been ideal for this book to have covered the whole of Exmoor in the frost and snow but it simply couldn't be done and that in itself is part of the picture of winter I was shown – that roads simply become impassable and five feet of snow is impossible to walk on. Hills become impossible to ascend or descend; shops, businesses and people all run out of things and people stay put. On the other hand, people talk to each other and help each other. All the normal restrictions are suspended and people invite you into their homes and lives.

These pictures represent my journey through this winter. But I would urge anyone to go out on to Exmoor in the winter, get cold, get warm again and visit the events I visited and finish the season with a whole different perspective on winter and Christmas.

Neville Stanikk
2009

Brief dawn light illuminates bare trees whilst the fog lowers behind on to Five Burrows Hill.

No leaves on the trees below Wheddon Cross but winter has yet to set in.

The village of Wheddon Cross in the winter sunshine. If there's any snow on Exmoor, it's Wheddon Cross that gets it!

Extraordinary cloud formation
above Wilmersham Common.

Winter mist in Luscombe Plantation.

Ice formed during the night in a puddle alongside the River Barle at Simonsbath.

Dead bracken coats the slopes of Trentishoe Down.

Only a few leaves near the ground remain in the woods in the Heddon Valley.

Ferns in Heddon Valley Woods.

After a cold night,
steam rises in the
morning sunshine in
Heddon Valley Woods.

Sheep on the northern slopes of Trentishoe Down.

(Right)
Frost-covered tree stump below Simonsbath marks the first frost of the winter.

River Barle below Simonsbath, just after dawn.

Frost lingers in the shadows at Daddy Combe.

River Barle looking upstream towards Simonsbath.

Shadowed hill and rocky outcrop at Flexbarrow.

The remains of Wheal Eliza, a disused copper mine at Flexbarrow.

Every year, on the first Saturday in December, Lynton has its late night Christmas shopping evening. Every shop is open and customers and performers fill the streets.

Frost on stone in the early morning light.

Looking like something from an electron microscope, frost fringes a stone fallen from a wall.

The River Barle upstream from Cow Castle.

Morning sunlight illuminates a bare willow tree near Cow Castle.

Reflections of sunlight on the River Barle.

Dry stone wall on Flexbarrow.

Reflections of sunlit bracken in the shallows of the River Barle.

(Right)
Frost fringes the vertical stones atop a dry stone wall.

The cold blue water of the River Barle catches a tiny reflection of the sunlit hills above.

Ice forming in bars across a hole in the mud. One of many bizarre forms that ice seems able to take.

Christmas Past:
The First Christmas
Doors

(Left)
The Christmas Tree Festival in the Methodist church, Minehead. Dozens of Christmas trees are decorated by different organisations in aid of charity.

Frost-covered beech leaves at Wheddon Cross.

Lanterns at Dunster by Candlelight.

(Right)
Shepherds come to visit the baby Jesus – or at least it could be. Spectators listen to musicians playing in the Yarnmarket at Dunster by Candlight.

Yarn Market

Attended by thousands, Dunster by Candlelight is a two evening event in December, with every shop open and dozens of events taking place.

Stile on North Molton Ridge.

The last rays of a winter sun catch North Hill at Minehead.

Frosty heather on
Withypool Common.

Dawn breaks across Withypool Common.

Frosty dawn at Withypool.

Icicles beside the road at Withypool.

Frost coats every leaf on this morning at Withypool.

The Barle Valley below Withypool.

Cottages at Withypool with Withypool Common behind.

Frosty morning at Exford.

Overwhelmingly pink dawn at Long Holcombe.

Freezing sea fog envelopes Dunkery Beacon.

Horner in deep and freezing shadow.

Hailstones on Brendon Common.

(Right)
Ice-covered tree and woods at Culbone Hill.

Brendon Common after
a hailstorm.

Frosty dawn at Simonsbath, looking down the River Barle.

Exmoor pony mother and foal.

Candlelit window in Molland parish church.

Carols by Candlelight at Molland. With so many candles and no electric lighting, the quality of the light becomes incandescent.

(Right)
The Blue Ball Inn at Countisbury.

The
BLUE BALL
INN
THE BLUE BALL INN

Another of the varied structures that
ice can take.

(Left)
After heavy rain, water seeping out of
the ground has frozen on the surface as
a sea of ice.

(Left)
Another example, this time looking like a thick fluid.

Exmoor ponies on Molland Common.

Light frost at Dane's
Brook by Lower
Willingford Bridge.

First snow of the winter on Brendon Common.

Scottish Blackface sheep huddle together against the wind on Brendon Common.

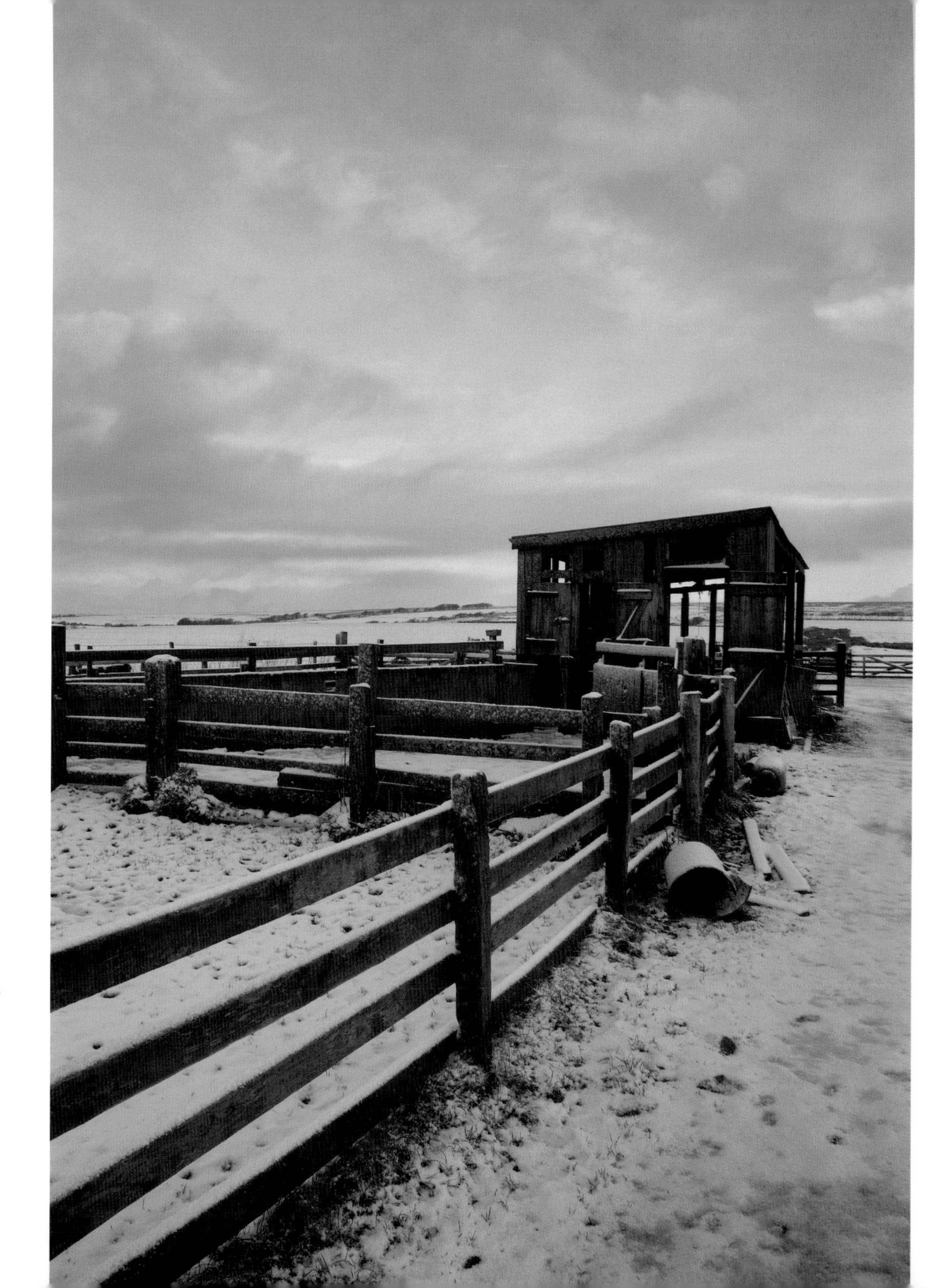

A dusting of snow on sheep pens near Simonsbath.

Heavy snow clouds over Brendon Common.

Snow clouds build up behind a gate on Dure Down.

A break in the snow gives a lone sheep the chance to peer out from behind trees on Alderman's Barrow Allotment.

(Left) Receding snowstorm on Goat Hill, west of Simonsbath.

Icy slush at Woolcombe Allotment.

Dawn over South Regis Common.

(Left)
Snowy, sunny morning at Blue Gate.

Clovenrocks Wood with a dusting of snow.

The beach and bay at Combe Martin.

Combe Martin from the hills, looking out to sea.

Westleigh Farm, below Nutcombe Hill, Combe Martin.

Snow on bags of silage with Nutcombe Hill in the distance.

Hedge near
Challacombe.

Looking north east from Kentisbury Down.

Tracks in the snow near Combe Martin.

Valley of the Rocks, with South Cleave on the right.

Snow on The Castle,
Valley of the Rocks.

The Castle and Exmoor coastline from South Cleave, Valley of the Rocks.

Foreland Point from Eastern Beach at Lynmouth.

A deserted Lynmouth in the snow – probably because of the difficulty of using either Lynmouth Hill or Countisbury Hill to get there!

The East Lyn River at Watersmeet.

(Right)
Evening sunlight falls on Horner's Neck Woods as the East Lyn River lies in shadow at Watersmeet.

Granulated snow created by a snow plough.

Watersmeet House and the East Lyn River.

Snowdrift at Breakneck Hole.

(Right)
Bypassed length of road at Breakneck Hole.

South Regis Common from North Lane, east of Challacombe.

Looking south west from North Lane, east of Challacombe.

North Lane, near Challacombe.

Snowdrift at Breakneck Hole.

Snowdrift at Breakneck Hole with South Regis Common in the distance.

The road into
Challacombe.

(Left)
The centre of Breakneck Hole is a bit of a dumping ground (look closely for a couple of old tyres) but the snow has turned it into a winter wonderland.

Bypassed length of road at Breakneck Hole.

Windblown and snow-covered branches near Culbone.

The deepest snow of the winter – higher than a five bar gate – at Coulsworthy.

View to Heale Down and Trentishoe Down from Rowley Down.

Woody Bay Station.

The village of Parracombe.

Dunkery Beacon from Porlock Hill.

Hills at sunset near Dean, Barbrook.

All Saints' parish church, Dulverton.

The ubiquitous farmer's quad bike as life tries to carry on around heavy snow in Dulverton.

A watery winter sun casts pale shadows on Winsford Hill.

Snow drifts on Winsford Hill.

People await their turn to be pulled around the village green at Exford.

Almost furry, the valley and stream leading to Pinkery Pond.

'Sledging' above Old Close Bottom, Challacombe.

More 'sledging' near Challacombe. No sledges in sight but as this is also in North Devon, plenty of bodyboards – many broken by the end of the day.

(Left)
Ashton Cleave and Southern Wood
from County Gate.

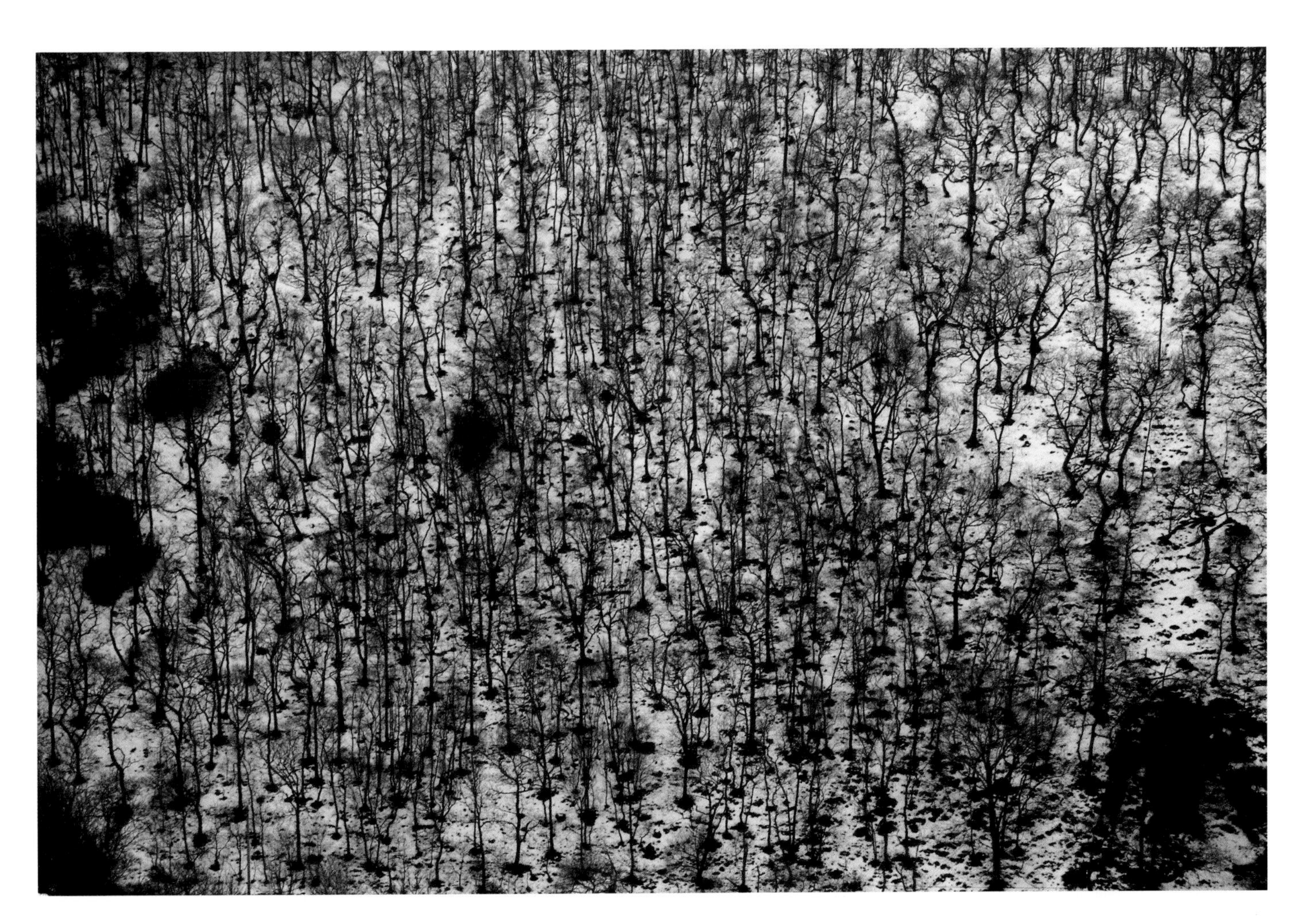

Bare trees in Southern Wood as seen
from County Gate.

Looking towards Ashton Cleave from Leeford.

The bridge and ford at Malmsmead.

Lorna Doone Farm shop at Malmsmead.

St Peter's church, Oare.

Oaremead Farm near Malsmead.

No shadows under a white sky at Hawcombe Head.

Dunkery Beacon from Alderman's Barrow Allotment.

View west from Exford Common.

Winsford in the snow.

Snow-covered graveyard at Exford parish church.

Footsteps in the snow at
Yenworthy Common.

Deep winter snow at Wheddon Cross.

Late afternoon snowy field at Wheddon Cross. The last snow of the winter, a pile of snow in the car park at Wheddon Cross, took ten days to melt despite the sun shining for most of that time.

(Right)
The first signs of spring – snowdrops in Snowdrop Valley, Wheddon Cross.

Snowdrops carpet the ground at Snowdrop Valley, Wheddon Cross.

(Left)
Melting snow at Robber's Bridge.

(Left)
Crocuses bloom in the churchyard
of Exford parish church.

Lambs in their plastic macs – used if the lambs are to be in the fields early.
Not to keep the lambs warm but to keep them dry.

Crocuses in the churchyard at Arlington.

(Right)
The kindly face of an Exmoor Horn sheep.

Hounds of the Exmoor Foxhounds.

(Right)
The Exmoor Foxhounds hold a lawn meet at Pickedstones Farm.

Hounds of the Devon & Somerset Staghounds.

(Left)
March, and the weather starts to warm up. No green yet but definitely hazy weather at Cornham Brake.

Riders of the Devon & Exmoor Staghounds set off from the Market Field at Wheddon Cross.

A Scottish Blackface sheep in the gorse on Malmsmead Hill.

And with daffodils and sunshine, spring arrives in full force at Selworthy.